Sports Innovations

INNOVATIONS IN AUTO RACING

by Douglas Hustad

SportsZone

An Imprint of Abdo Publishing
abdobooks.com

abdobooks.com

Published by Abdo Publishing, a division of ABDO, PO Box 398166, Minneapolis, Minnesota 55439. Copyright © 2022 by Abdo Consulting Group, Inc. International copyrights reserved in all countries. No part of this book may be reproduced in any form without written permission from the publisher. SportsZone™ is a trademark and logo of Abdo Publishing.

Printed in the United States of America, North Mankato, Minnesota.
102021
012022

THIS BOOK CONTAINS
RECYCLED MATERIALS

Cover Photos: Russell LaBounty/NKP/AP Images, left; AP Images, right
Interior Photos: RacingOne/ISC Archives/Getty Images, 5; LK/AP Images, 7; Grindstone Media Group/Shutterstock Images, 8, 38–39; National Motor Museum/Heritage Images/ Hulton Archive/Getty Images, 11; Photo Works/Shutterstock Images, 13; Chris O'Meara/ AP Images, 14, 31; Brian Horton/AP Images, 17; Paul-Henri Cahier/Hulton Archive/Getty Images, 18; David Madison/Getty Images Sport/Getty Images, 20; Kyodo/AP Images, 21; Mikhail Kolesnikov/Shutterstock Images, 23; Shutterstock Images, 24, 26, 34; Plamen Denov/Shutterstock Images, 29; Rainier Ehrhardt/AP Images, 32–33; AP Images, 37; Matthew T. Thacker/NKP/AP Images, 41; Chris Trotman/Getty Images Sport/Getty Images, 43

Editor: Katie Chanez
Series Designer: Joshua Olson

Library of Congress Control Number: 2020949103

Publisher's Cataloging-in-Publication Data

Names: Hustad, Douglas, author.
Title: Innovations in auto racing / by Douglas Hustad
Description: Minneapolis, Minnesota : Abdo Publishing, 2022 | Series: Sports innovations | Includes online resources and index.
Identifiers: ISBN 9781532195013 (lib. bdg.) | ISBN 9781098215323 (ebook)
Subjects: LCSH: Automobile racing--Juvenile literature. | Technological innovations-- Juvenile literature. | Sports sciences--Juvenile literature. | Performance technology--Juvenile literature. | Sports cars--Juvenile literature. | Sports--Juvenile literature.
Classification: DDC 688.76--dc23

TABLE OF
CONTENTS

CHAPTER 1

THE RISE OF
NASCAR

Stock car racing started where the road ran out. In the 1930s and '40s, automobile enthusiasts brought their cars to Daytona Beach, Florida, to test them on the sand against other daredevils' cars. The vehicles looked like normal road cars, but their drivers had lovingly turned them into race cars.

The beach course ran 2 miles (3.2 km) up and down the coast. Spectators flocked to the sidelines of the course. It gave Bill France an idea.

France convened a meeting on December 14, 1947. He gathered the organizers of these races. Together they formed a new organization: the National Association for Stock Car Auto Racing (NASCAR).

The "stock" in stock car means a car that is unmodified from the factory. In reality these cars started as regular road

caption: The first races at Daytona took place on the beach itself, not on a formal track.

cars, but had been heavily modified for racing. Still, they were far different from Formula One (F1) or Indy cars, which were open-wheel vehicles built specifically for racing.

FROM SMALL BEGINNINGS

A crowd of 13,000 came out to watch the first NASCAR Strictly Stock series race on June 19, 1949. The race lasted 200 laps at Charlotte Speedway in North Carolina. First place came with a prize of $2,000.

NASCAR continued to hold races on Daytona Beach. By 1959 Daytona International Speedway opened. It was a 2.5-mile (4 km) paved track where tens of thousands of people could watch the races. The stock car series was becoming a smashing success.

By the 1970s, certain races attracted hundreds of thousands of people. Fans rooted for their favorite drivers. Stock car racing became the most popular form of auto racing in the United States.

Cars gradually became less and less like their everyday road counterparts. By the 1980s, only the body panels from road

NOT JUST RED, WHITE, AND BLUE

NASCAR has historically been a US series with US manufacturers. But foreign automakers such as Porsche, Jaguar, and MG have entered cars. Toyota became the first foreign car maker to win a championship in 2016.

Early stock cars looked more like regular road cars than the stock cars of today.

cars made it onto race cars. By 1992 even these were gone, and the cars were specifically built for racing. Cars feature a body formed from a single piece of metal on top of a custom-built chassis. Cars were also made to be the same size as one another to ensure nobody had an unfair advantage.

Modern stock cars are still designed to look like road cars, even though they are custom built for racing.

OLD TECH, SAME THRILLS

NASCAR today is a unique form of racing. Unlike other series such as F1, where the emphasis is on adapting to the latest trends in technology, NASCAR likes to stick to its roots whenever possible.

That means NASCAR racers are big, heavy machines. They weigh more than 3,000 pounds (1,360 kg). F1 cars are roughly half that weight. Stock cars run on a four-speed manual transmission. Their V8 engines are the same basic design as they were in the 1950s.

Yet NASCAR stock cars go well over 200 miles per hour (322 km/h). They provide thrilling races almost every Sunday. And it all started on a beach in Florida.

CHAPTER 2

SAFETY FIRST

The first recorded auto race began in Paris, France, on July 22, 1894. It took the winner six hours and 48 minutes to reach the finish line, which was 79 miles (127 km) away in the town of Rouen. He averaged 12 miles per hour (19 km/h). At those leisurely speeds, safety wasn't much of a concern.

Auto racing developed quickly, and so did its related dangers. By the early 1900s, cars raced at speeds over 80 miles per hour (129 km/h). Safety efforts were minimal and failed to keep pace with other racing developments. Taking risks was just an accepted part of the sport. Even into the 1950s, dozens of professional drivers were killed each year.

The risks were high for fans, too. Races were mostly run on streets instead of specially designed racetracks. Barriers between spectators and the racers were few and far between. At the 24-hour race in Le Mans, France, in 1955, 80 people were

caption: **Twenty-one cars raced between Paris and Rouen in 1894, but only 17 reached the finish line.**

killed by debris flying into the crowd following a crash.

THE SAFETY GUY

Bill Simpson knew the risks as well as anyone. In 1958, at age 18, he broke both arms in a racing accident. Like most drivers, he didn't think much about safety until he had an accident. It was serious enough that safety remained a priority of his even after he got back behind the wheel.

Simpson continued his racing career, but he also founded a company dedicated to making safety equipment. Simpson used the material Nomex to make fireproof driving suits. Nomex was previously used to make astronaut suits. To prove his suit worked, Simpson lit himself on fire in a 1980s advertisement. Simpson's company made other equipment, including helmets and seat belts.

Better equipment made racing a lot safer. But crashes that claimed the lives of some legendary drivers changed the sport forever. Three-time F1 world champion Ayrton Senna died in a crash in 1994. F1 made drastic changes. Cars were designed

NASCAR drivers and pit crew members wear helmets and fire suits to keep them safe.

to better protect drivers. Tracks were redesigned to minimize danger. In the 25 years after the accident, F1 didn't lose a single driver during a race weekend.

DEATH SHAKES NASCAR

In the United States, the death of Dale Earnhardt shocked the NASCAR community. Earnhardt was a seven-time NASCAR

NASCAR drivers wear HANS devices to protect them in case of an accident.

series champion. In the 2001 Daytona 500, NASCAR's biggest race, Earnhardt's car was hit from behind. It spun out of control and rocketed toward the outer wall. His car hit the wall at 150 miles per hour (241 km/h), and he was killed instantly.

NASCAR had already planned to make safety changes. Earnhardt, for example, was still wearing an old-fashioned helmet without a face shield. His death prompted some changes to be implemented in a hurry.

All drivers were soon required to wear a Head and Neck Restraint System (HANS). The HANS device is a collar the driver wears that restricts the movement of a driver's head. This keeps the head from whipping around in a wreck.

NASCAR also changed the tracks. Steel and Foam Energy (SAFER) Barriers were added to outside retaining walls. These walls were softer than concrete and absorbed energy better. This made crashes less dangerous.

NASCAR also made other rule changes over the years, such as adding flaps on a car's roof to keep it from flying up in the air. These changes greatly reduced the number of driver deaths. Racing is still dangerous, but not nearly as dangerous as it once was.

CHAPTER 3

PADDLING

FORWARD

For nearly a century, nearly every racing driver changed gears the same way: Press in the clutch pedal, and change gears with the shift lever. Manual transmissions improved over the years, becoming more durable and able to shift faster. But the mechanics didn't change much.

In cars that use automatic transmission, the engine changes gears on its own. Those transmissions were common in road cars for decades. But they hadn't been introduced to the racing world. However, in the mid-1980s, the Ferrari F1 race team was experimenting with a semi-automatic transmission. In that system, the driver still changed the gears. But he did not have to use a clutch pedal. The shifts would happen much faster and increase acceleration.

caption:

Before the 1980s, all racing cars had manual transmissions. Drivers had to use a shift lever to change gears.

Ferrari technical designer John Barnard, *left*, works with driver Gerhard Berger, who was on the first racing team to use the semi-automatic transmission.

A PEDAL TO A PADDLE

Ferrari encountered many problems designing the system. It failed often. Drivers didn't trust it. Finally in 1988, engineers made one that worked.

Previous designs still included a shift lever. The driver would push it forward or backward to change gears. Ferrari technical director John Barnard had a better idea. He proposed putting two buttons on the steering wheel. This design evolved into having two paddles behind the wheel. This allowed drivers to keep both hands fully on the wheel.

A third paddle acted as a clutch. Drivers only had to use this to start the engine. The clutch engaged automatically for gear changes.

The semi-automatic transmission debuted in the 1989 season. Driver Nigel Mansell used it to win in his first race in Brazil. That was the start of a roller coaster year for the vehicle. When the car finished, it was fast—Mansell and teammate Gerhard Berger won three races and finished in the top three six other times. But in almost every other race, the car broke down and didn't finish. Not all failures were due to the transmission, but there were still some fixes to be made.

Despite the problems encountered that first year, it signaled the start of a revolution. By 1996 every F1 team had eliminated the standard manual transmission. And other series were starting to change over, too. IndyCar went to paddle shifters

NO SHIFTING HERE

Most major auto racing series require drivers to change gears. The top level of drag racing is one exception. There simply isn't time. Cars race each other over 1,000 feet (305 m). Top Fuel and Funny Car dragsters run this distance in under four seconds. Gear changes happen automatically based on timing.

Nigel Mansell drove one of the first F1 cars with a semi-automatic transmission. He had some successes, but the car struggled with mechanical problems.

in 2008. One notable holdout was NASCAR, which kept its same 4-speed manual gearbox.

LIGHTNING FAST

Semi-automatic transmissions continued to get lighter and faster. These transmissions are amazing pieces of technology. They start when the driver moves the paddle. A control unit then checks the engine speed. It opens the clutch. The gear then actually changes. The control unit makes sure the gears are all lined up. Then it closes the clutch.

This all happens in 10-15 milliseconds. A 90-mph (145 km/h) fastball takes approximately 400 milliseconds to reach home plate. A blink of an eye takes 300.

And the technology isn't just used in race cars. Ferrari began putting paddle shifters on its road cars soon after it implemented them in its F1 racers. Today, they are a common feature of many road cars.

All F1 cars still use semi-automatic transmissions. Drivers can use their ability to shift gears at the right moment to gain an advantage in a race.

GOING GREEN

Electric and hybrid cars began to appear on roads and in driveways in the 1990s. These cars were better for the environment but not all that fun to drive. It was hard to make a car that had a lot of power that didn't also burn a lot of gas.

It was even harder to strike that balance in a race car, though there was never a need to do so. Racing emissions are not regulated by the government or by racing circuits. The cars don't have to pass government inspections. So for years, there wasn't much reason to make changes.

But technology started to catch up. What if automakers could build a car that ran more efficiently and produced just as much power? That would be a no-brainer.

KERS

Formula One cars began using a Kinetic Energy Recovery System (KERS) in 2009. All teams were using it by 2013.

caption:

The US government does not regulate emissions created by race cars. However, many circuits are working to reduce their impact on the environment.

KERS uses energy created by F1 cars to reduce the amount of fuel each car uses.

KERS takes advantage of energy F1 cars generate while braking. Without KERS, this energy is lost as heat. KERS captures this energy to be used again.

When an F1 car brakes, the energy is transferred to a flywheel. This wheel spins and charges a battery with the energy. The energy is stored there until the driver needs it. A push of a button adds that power to the energy the engine creates.

KERS can add up to 80 horsepower for up to seven seconds per lap. That can be a huge boost for a driver trying to make a pass. Instead of the engine burning more fuel for energy to make up that difference, KERS can use energy that would otherwise be lost. That means KERS is more efficient and better for the environment. By the 2020 season, energy recovery on cars had evolved from just the KERS system to a dual energy recovery system (ERS). Cars had an updated version of KERS and also a system that took waste heat and turned it into energy.

FORMULA E

The International Automobile Federation operates other race series besides F1. In 2014 it launched Formula E. This was a racing series exclusively for electric cars. These race cars can reach top speeds of 174 miles per hour (280 km/h).

GREEN GAS

Race cars usually run on special fuel. It is designed to help engines create more power than the gas available at regular pumps. But engineers found a way to make a fuel for stock cars that was better for the environment with no drop-off in power.

In 2011 NASCAR began using a fuel partially made from ethanol. Ethanol is a biofuel. It is made from corn. Ethanol is then blended with regular racing fuel for NASCAR. The mix is 85 percent racing fuel and 15 percent ethanol. That may not sound like a lot. But it lowers emissions by 20 percent.

Biofuels are made from many types of plants including wheat and sugar cane. NASCAR's ethanol blend is made from corn.

Cars are no slower running on the ethanol blend. Some teams even reported an increase in horsepower using ethanol. They began testing fuels that had double the percentage of ethanol. NASCAR was still using the 15 percent blend into the 2020 season.

LOWERING CARBON FOOTPRINT

Race cars aren't the only vehicles in a racing series that burn fuel. Series such as F1 travel all over the globe each year. That requires a fleet of planes and trucks carrying the crews to where they are needed.

In 2019 F1 took steps to become carbon neutral by 2030. A carbon footprint is a measure of how much pollution a person, group, or object adds to the environment. Carbon neutrality means leaving no footprint at all.

F1 discussed many steps to reach its goal. It planned to recycle or compost all waste at racetracks by 2025. And it mandated that by 2021 cars had to run on at least 10 percent biofuels.

CHAPTER 5

ALL ABOUT
THE AERO

More power means more speed. That was clear in auto racing from the beginning. It also made sense that the sleeker a car was, the better it cut through the air. But engineers didn't figure out until later that aerodynamics could help in other ways. If a car was pressed to the ground, it had better traction. If it had better traction, more of its power went to the road.

NASCAR teams were reaching the limits of engine design in the 1960s. Racing engines were about as powerful as they could be under the rules. That was when teams really started to study aerodynamics. This set off an era called the Aero Wars in the late 1960s and early '70s.

In that era of NASCAR, the stock cars on the track had more in common with regular cars on the road. Each manufacturer had to sell similar cars to the public in order to race them

caption:

NASCAR engines are innovative machines. Engineers combined powerful engines with aerodynamics to help increase the cars' speed.

SAE 30R7 Not For Fuel Injection Systems

in NASCAR. Ford and Chrysler went back and forth making new cars that were more aerodynamic.

The problem was they were too aerodynamic. They were too fast to be driven safely. In 1970 Buddy Baker became the first NASCAR driver to go 200 miles per hour (322 km/h). The cars traveled faster than the tires could handle. In response, NASCAR changed its rules to limit engine size. That meant the cars' aerodynamic advantage was eliminated.

RACING FORCES

Teams eventually figured out how to use aerodynamics more safely. Every race team is looking for downforce. Downforce is the force that pushes the car down on the track. The more air that pushes a car down, the more traction the car gets. But teams don't want too much downforce. They also need their car to cut through the air to maximize its speed.

Race cars have spoilers on the back. The spoiler sticks up from the car and catches air. The air that pushes on the spoiler creates downforce. When another car approaches from behind, the air pushes up and over both cars. This is called drafting. Because the trailing car doesn't have to create its own downforce, it uses less energy.

Drivers use drafting to gain speed and improve fuel efficiency.

However, drafting can make cars unstable. The trailing car has less downforce on the front of the car. This is where the steering is done. Less traction on those wheels makes cars harder to handle.

The best drivers learn how to balance these forces to maximize efficiency and control. Teams test their cars in wind tunnels to observe how air affects them. They test drive their vehicles extensively. Even a tiny fraction of an inch can make a huge difference on how the car drives.

Drafting can happen in packs. If one car bumps into another, it can cause accidents.

That is why NASCAR and other series enforce rules so tightly. NASCAR makes rules to ensure a fair competition. Each team's car must follow these rules. Cars are checked before and after a race. Every inch is examined to make sure the car is within the limits. Teams that don't pass the inspection have

to make adjustments to comply with the rules before they can race. And they may be docked a starting position or points at the finish.

F1 GETS ITS WINGS

F1 cars make about 1,000 horsepower. But what really makes them super machines is aerodynamics. An F1 car has

Spoilers at the front and back of F1 cars create downforce so drivers don't lose control at high speeds.

two spoilers. One is at the front, and one is at the back. These spoilers are shaped like airplane wings. Only instead of creating lift, these press the car down.

The downforce for F1 cars must be perfectly balanced. Unlike NASCAR tracks that are mostly oval-shaped, F1 tracks include turns in both directions. When the car turns, the downforce must be balanced between the front and back of the car. F1 cars all look roughly the same. But each team can make small adjustments to make their cars handle perfectly.

Fans turn out to see big, powerful engines. But the science of aerodynamics is really what makes racing so exciting.

DRIVING ON THE CEILING

F1 cars generate a lot of downforce. They generate so much, in fact, that the force pushing down on them is greater than the weight of the car. This means that, in theory, an F1 car would be capable of driving upside down on the ceiling.

CHAPTER 6

ON TRACK

Indiana businessman Carl Fisher was a racing fan from the early days. He watched races in France in 1905 and saw how advanced racing in Europe had become. Fisher wanted the same thing in the United States. But the tracks of the era were not well suited for racing. Races often took place on public roads. Not only were they dangerous, but fans could not get a good view. They had to wait for the cars to come by and only saw them for a brief period.

Fisher suggested building a circular track. Such tracks already existed, such as Brooklands in the United Kingdom. Fisher visited Brooklands and was even more excited to build his track.

Fisher's idea became Indianapolis Motor Speedway. It was 2.5 miles (4 km) and shaped like an oval. It became one of the most famous racetracks in the world. It opened in 1909. In 1911

caption: **Carl Fisher developed the Indianapolis Motor Speedway in the early 1900s.**

As of 2020, the Indianapolis Motor Speedway was the largest sporting venue in the world. It can seat more than 200,000 people.

it began hosting one of the world's most famous races, the Indianapolis 500.

The Indy 500 may have been the world's most famous race on an oval track. But the rest of the season, Indycars ran

mostly on road courses. F1 ran completely on road courses. As NASCAR emerged in the 1950s, it made oval racing popular.

THE OVAL BOOM

The first NASCAR season ran on existing racetracks. But in 1950, the first track built for the series held its first race. NASCAR has been racing at Darlington Raceway in South Carolina ever since.

Darlington was also the first fully paved track on the NASCAR schedule. All others were at least partially covered by dirt.

Daytona International Speedway opened in 1959. That same year, the Daytona 500 had its first race. It is the only US race to rival the Indy 500 in popularity. The Daytona 500 has been held ever since.

NASCAR tracks were built with high degrees of banking in the turns. This meant the cars did not have to slow down as much. That made for thrilling racing. Cars could run close together at speeds over 200 miles per hour (322 km/h).

The IndyCar series began to run more ovals in the 1990s. These powerful cars drove faster than 200 miles per hour (322 km/h). But by the late 2010s, the series was going back to more road courses. NASCAR, meanwhile, typically runs just two or three road courses per year.

A SMOOTH SURFACE

Dirt racing remains popular in smaller series. But the days of dirt racing for the top series are long gone. Tracks are now paved with the latest in pavement technology. The high bankings are a challenge. The pavement mix must be carried uphill to the paver. Bulldozers sit at the top of the turn to keep the paver steady.

NASCAR tracks are famous for their high bankings. The turns at Daytona International Speedway have a 31-degree banking.

A racetrack is quite different from a normal highway. The pavement is mixed with a material that is similar to Styrofoam. This helps it to stay firm under hot racing tires. It's also very dense. The track is so dense, it doesn't absorb water. Water is the enemy of a racetrack. Stock cars cannot run in wet conditions. The tires would get no grip on a wet track. So when it rains, the race is delayed.

MEET THE TITAN

Drying the track is no easy task. In the past, races couldn't be held on rainy days. Then in the 1970s, tracks started to use jet dryers. The first one was created by Dan Salenbien at Michigan International Speedway. He took a jet engine and pointed the exhaust nozzle downward. Hot air blasted the surface of the track.

Jet dryers soon became common in NASCAR. But they weren't perfect. The hot air—over 1,100 degrees Fahrenheit (593°C)—could damage the track. And they were expensive to run. They used more than 12,000 gallons (45,000 L) of fuel to dry a track.

NASCAR now uses a system call the Air Titan. It was introduced before the 2013 season. Rather than very hot air, the Air Titan simply blows air at high speeds. It delivers air at 568 miles per hour (914 km/h). It could inflate the Goodyear Blimp in under four minutes.

Wet racetracks make driving dangerous. NASCAR uses dryers to keep tracks safe for drivers and avoid postponements.

It is also a much smaller system. Each one fits in the bed of a pickup truck. It takes eight trucks to dry a track like Daytona. The system is up to 80 percent faster than the old way.

There is hardly any part of modern auto racing that hasn't changed since the sport began. Auto racing is always innovating and looking for ways to get faster. Those changes help keep fans excited and keep drivers pushing the limits.

TIMELINE

1894
The first auto race is held in France, a 79-mile (127-km) journey from Paris to Rouen.

1909
Indianapolis Motor Speedway opens and becomes one of the first major oval raceways in the world.

1933
Five people are killed in the running of the Indianapolis 500, the deadliest weekend in the race's history, highlighting the need for safety improvements.

1947
Bill France founds the first major stock car auto racing series, called NASCAR, in Daytona Beach, Florida.

1958
Race car driver Bill Simpson breaks both arms in a crash. He later starts a company dedicated to safety equipment, and it ultimately invents the first fireproof racing suit.

1989
Ferrari runs the first semi-automatic transmission with paddle shifters in Formula One racing. By 1996 all F1 teams were running similar transmissions.

2001
NASCAR legend Dale Earnhardt dies in a crash at the Daytona 500. The series makes numerous safety improvements that spread to other racing series.

2009
The first Kinetic Energy Recovery System (KERS) is equipped to an F1 car.

2011
NASCAR mandates 15 percent ethanol fuel in an effort to cut down on greenhouse gas emissions.

2019
Formula One announces plans to become carbon neutral by 2030.

TIMING DATA

As vehicle speeds increased, it became harder and harder to time their laps accurately. Cars now carry sensors showing their exact position on the track. This has a benefit for fans too. They can always see where their favorite driver is in the running.

CARBON FIBER

A light material that was as strong as metal was the perfect fit for a race car. It came from aerospace research. The McLaren F1 team first used carbon fiber for an F1 chassis in 1981. The car was not only fast, it was safe. Carbon fiber protected drivers much better than aluminum. All F1 cars in 2020 have a carbon fiber chassis.

DRAG REDUCTION SYSTEM/PUSH-TO-PASS

Frequent passing is one thing that can make for an exciting race. Both IndyCar and F1 developed systems to increase passing. IndyCar's push-to-pass system temporarily increases the car's horsepower to provide a boost. In F1's Drag Reduction System (DRS), the rear wing flips to allow more air through and reduce downforce. Both systems have limits on how often the driver can use them.

GLOSSARY

aerodynamics
The study of how air moves over surfaces.

chassis
The basic frame of a car underneath the body.

clutch
A device that engages and disengages to allow for gear changes.

daredevils
People who enjoy doing risky or dangerous activities.

debris
Pieces that break off in an accident.

emissions
The fumes released by an engine as it runs.

gearbox
The housing inside of which gear changes take place.

horsepower
A measurement for how powerful an engine is.

hybrid
A vehicle powered by both a gas engine and electric motor.

open-wheel
A racing car whose wheels do not have any bodywork surrounding them.

transmission
The part of a car that takes power from the engine and transfers it to the wheels.

BOOKS

Marquardt, Meg. *STEM in Auto Racing*. Minneapolis, MN: Abdo Publishing, 2018.

Rule, Heather. *Ultimate NASCAR Road Trip*. Minneapolis, MN: Abdo Publishing, 2019.

Wilner, Barry. *The Best Auto Racers of All Time*. Minneapolis, MN: Abdo Publishing, 2015.

ONLINE RESOURCES

Booklinks
NONFICTION NETWORK
FREE! ONLINE NONFICTION RESOURCES

To learn more about innovations in auto racing, please visit **abdobooklinks.com** or scan this QR code. These links are routinely monitored and updated to provide the most current information available.

INDEX

ABOUT THE AUTHOR

Douglas Hustad is a freelance author primarily of science and history books for young people. He, his wife, and their two dogs live in the northern suburbs of San Diego, California.